P9-EED-504

The Solar System

Pluto

by Ralph Winrich

Consultant:
Stephen J. Kortenkamp, PhD
Research Scientist
Planetary Science Institute, Tucson, Arizona

Mankato, Minnesota

First Facts is published by Capstone Press,
151 Good Counsel Drive, P.O. Box 669, Mankato, Minnesota 56002.
www.capstonepress.com

Printed in the United States of America

Library of Congress Cataloging-in-Publication Data
Winrich, Ralph.
Pluto / by Ralph Winrich.
p. cm.—(First facts. The solar system)
Includes bibliographical references and index.
ISBN 0-7368-3693-4 (hardcover)
1. Pluto (Planet)—Juvenile literature. I. Title. II. First facts. Solar system.
QB701.W46 2005
523.482—dc22 2004016437

Summary: Discusses the orbit, atmosphere, surface features, and exploration of Pluto.

Editorial Credits
Gillia Olson, editor; Juliette Peters, designer and illustrator; Jo Miller, photo researcher;
Scott Thoms, photo editor

Photo Credits
The Johns Hopkins University Applied Physics Laboratory & Southwest Research Institute, 17
NASA, 9; Dr. R. Albrecht, ESA/ESO Space Telescope European Coordinating Facility, 5
NASA & ESA/Alan Stern (Southwest Research Institute), Marc Buie (Lowell Observatory), 16
Photodisc, planet images within illustrations and chart, 6–7, 19, 21
Photo Researchers Inc./Science Photo Library/Detlev Van Ravenswaay, cover, 14–15, 20

1 2 3 4 5 6 10 09 08 07 06 05

Table of Contents

The Farthest Planet

Pluto is the farthest planet from the Sun. **Spacecraft** haven't visited it yet. Today, the best pictures show Pluto as a fuzzy ball. Much about Pluto remains a mystery. Scientists make their best guesses about the planet. To draw Pluto, artists can use their imaginations.

Fast Facts about Pluto

Diameter: 1,440 miles (2,320 kilometers)
Average Distance from Sun: 3.7 billion miles (5.9 billion kilometers)
Average Temperature (surface): minus 382 degrees Fahrenheit (minus 230 degrees Celsius)
Length of Day: 6 Earth days, 9 hours, 17 minutes
Length of Year: 248 Earth years
Moons: 1

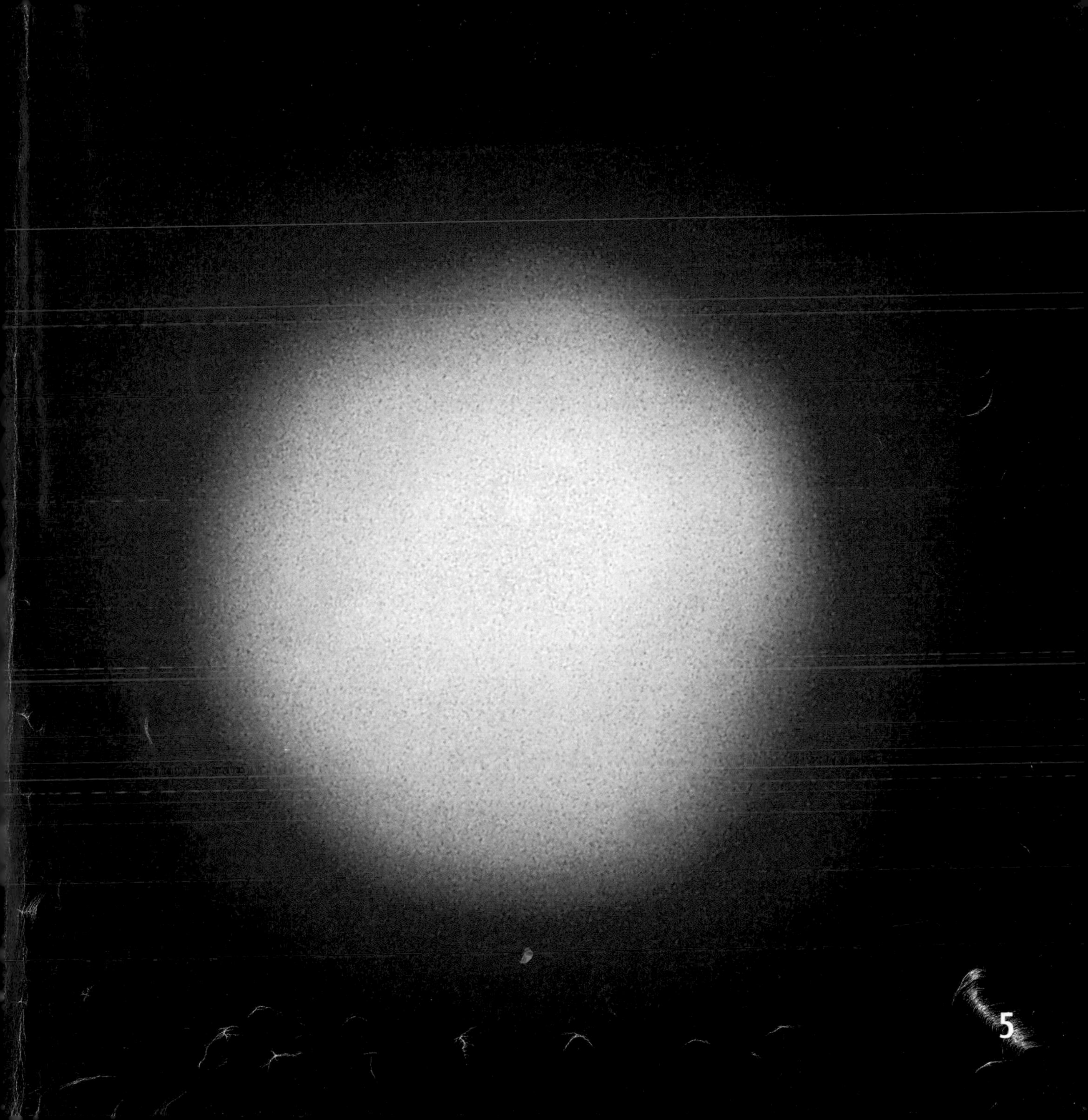

The Solar System

Pluto is the smallest planet in the solar system. It lies beyond the giant planets of Jupiter, Saturn, Uranus, and Neptune. The rocky planets of Mercury, Venus, Earth, and Mars are much smaller than the giant planets. Still, they are much larger than Pluto.

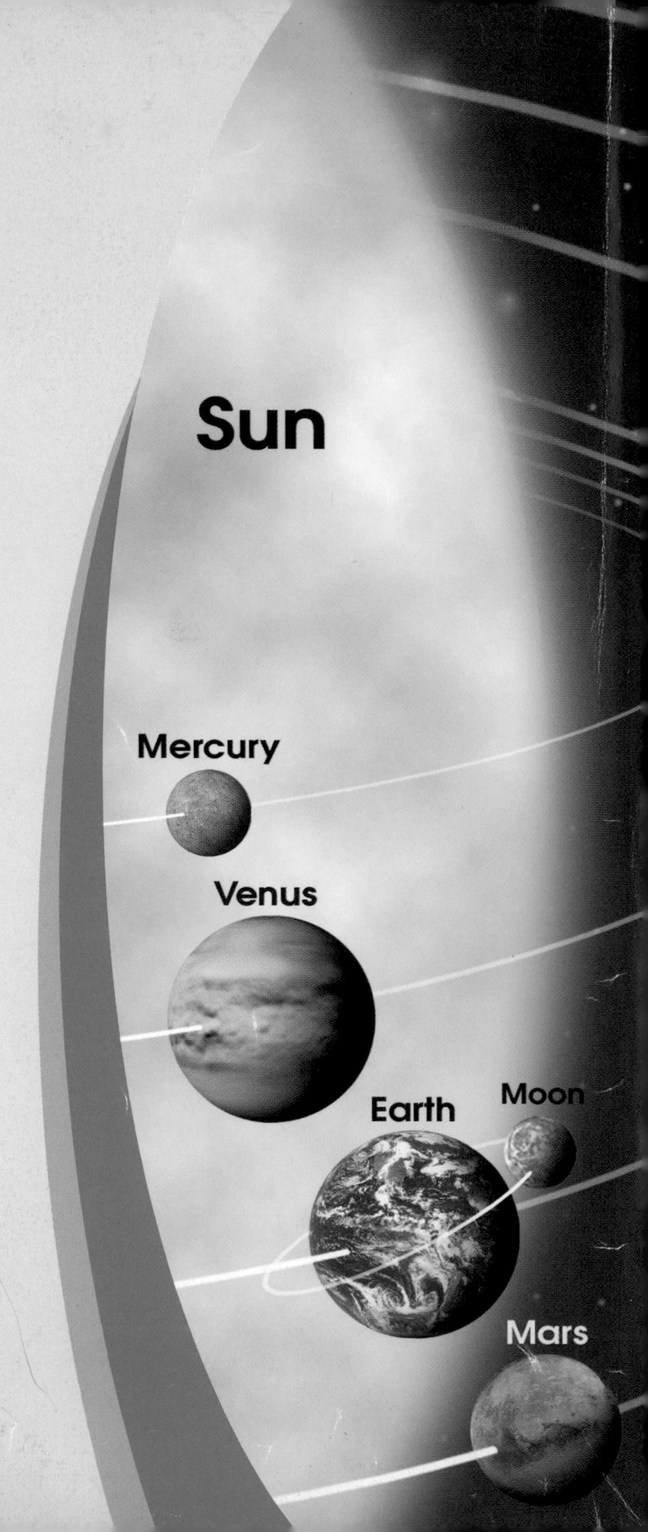

Jupiter
Pluto
Saturn
Uranus
Neptune

Pluto's Atmosphere

The gases surrounding a planet are called its **atmosphere**. Pluto's distance from the Sun affects its atmosphere. Pluto circles the Sun in an oval path. When closest to the Sun, its atmosphere is gas. When far from the Sun, the atmosphere freezes. It falls like snow onto the planet. Pluto then has no atmosphere.

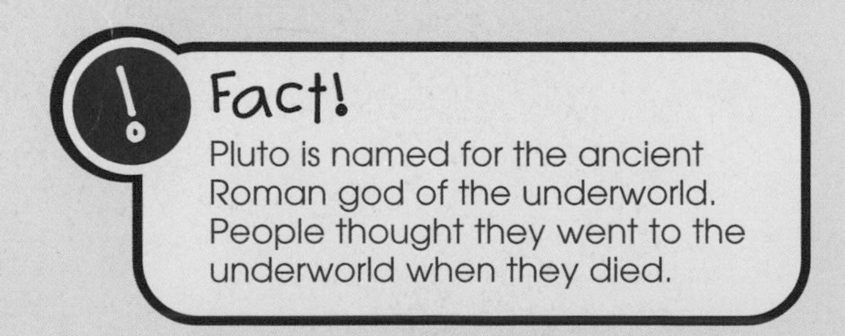

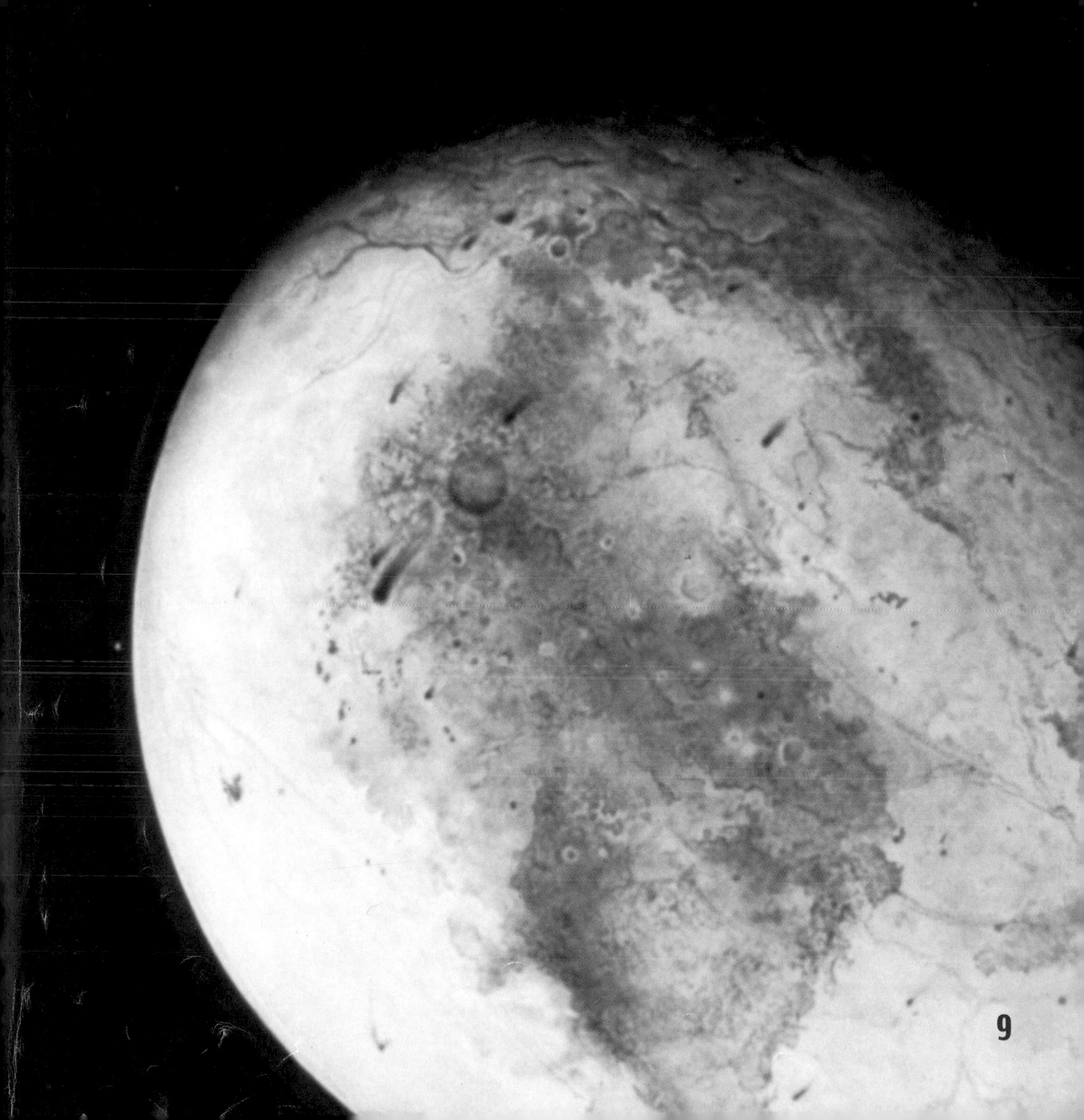

Pluto's Makeup

The surface, or **crust**, of Pluto is made up of ices. These ices are darker than water ice on Earth. They are made from nitrogen and methane mixed with water. Below Pluto's surface lies a thick **mantle** of water ice. The planet's **core** is rocky.

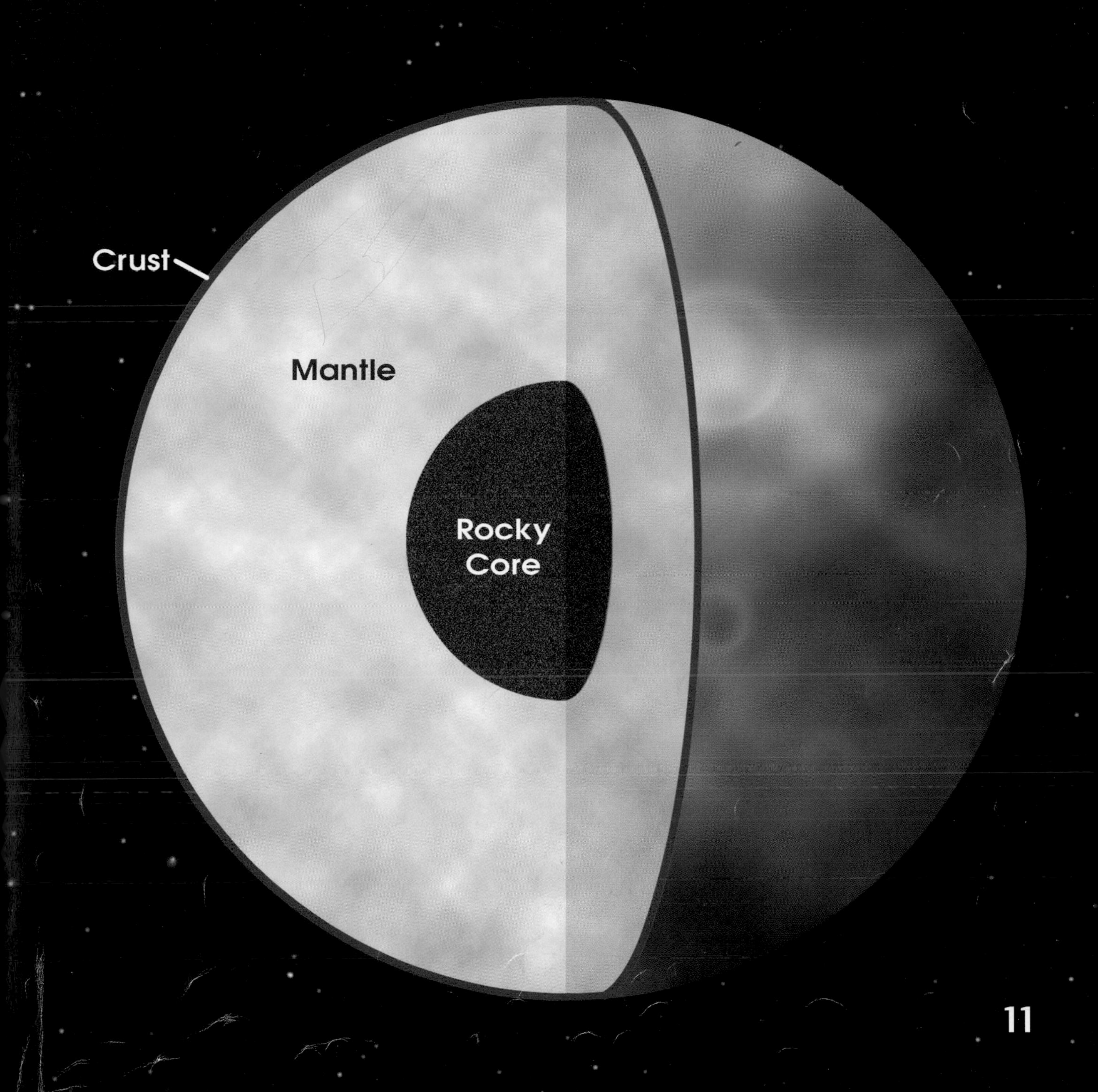
Crust
Mantle
Rocky
Core

Sun

Pluto

Axis

Path around the Sun

How Pluto Moves

Pluto travels around the Sun as it spins on its **axis**. Pluto takes 248 Earth years to move once around the Sun. It takes 6 days, 9 hours, 17 minutes to spin once.

Pluto spins the opposite direction of most planets. Venus is the only other planet that spins this way.

Pluto's Moon

Pluto has one moon, called Charon. Charon is about half the size of Pluto. Charon circles Pluto once in the same time as Pluto spins once. Charon and Pluto always keep the same sides facing each other.

Fact!

In the solar system, no other moon is as large compared to its planet as Charon is to Pluto.

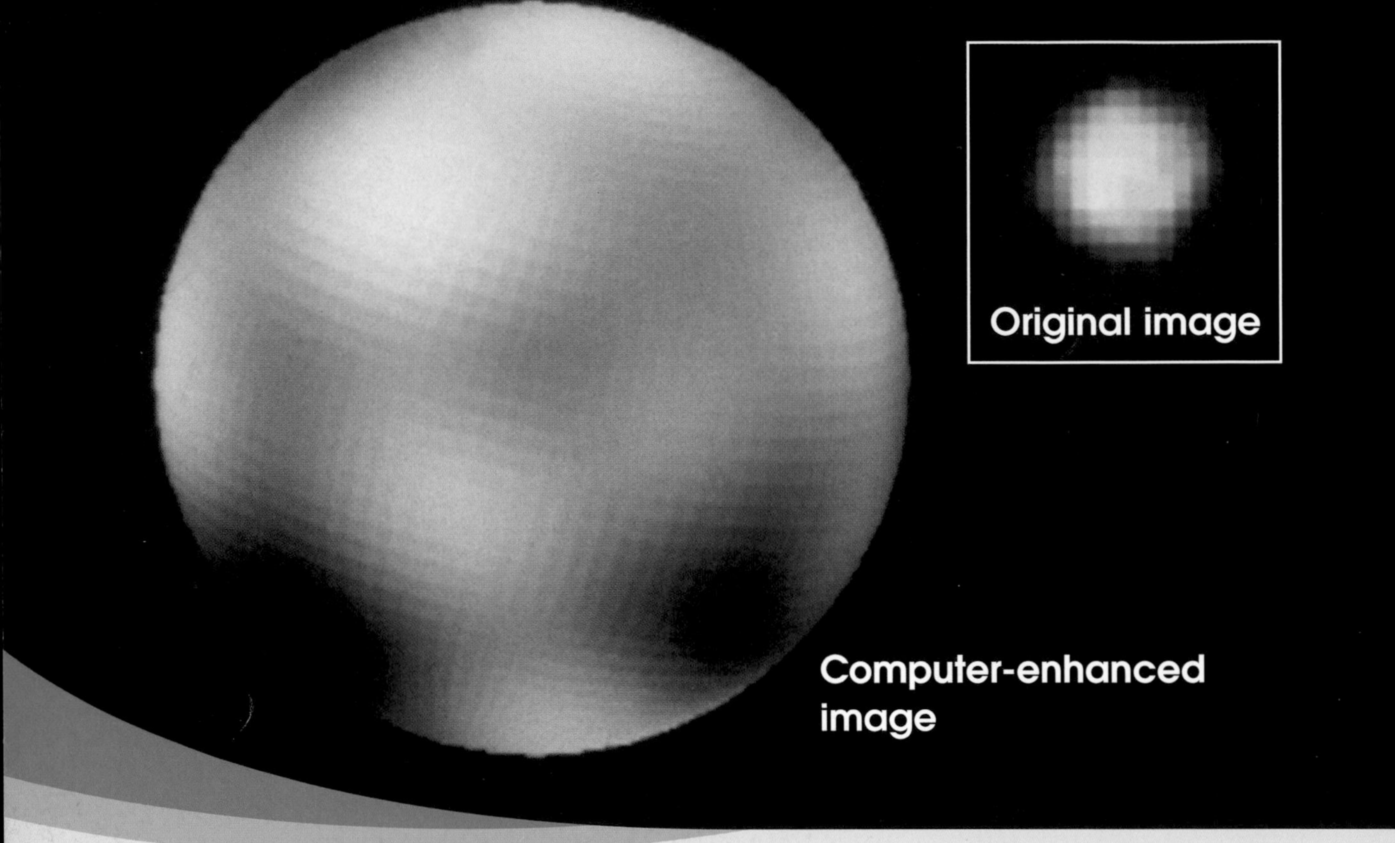

Studying Pluto

Even powerful **telescopes** show little detail of Pluto. They do show bright and dark surface areas. Scientists use computers to make the images clearer.

The spacecraft *New Horizons* will launch in 2006. It will fly by Pluto in 2015. It will take close-up pictures and gather information.

Comparing Pluto to Earth

Pluto and Earth are very different. Earth has a warm atmosphere. Sometimes, Pluto has no atmosphere. People could not live on cold, dark Pluto. But scientists will continue to study this mysterious planet.

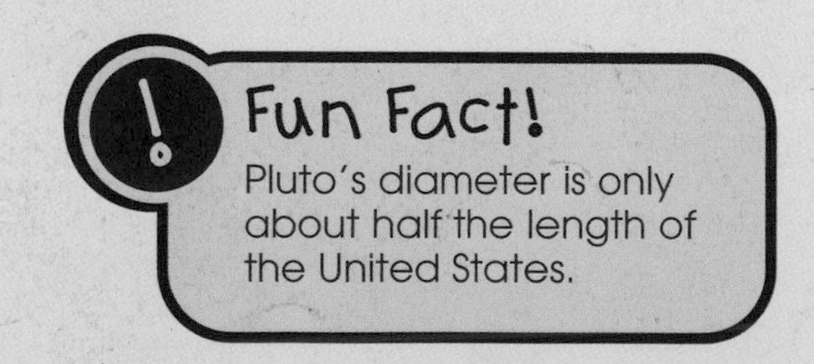

Size Comparison

Amazing but True!

Some scientists think Pluto isn't a planet. The solar system does not end at Pluto. Beyond Pluto, more than 700 objects that circle the Sun have been found. Some of these objects are almost as large as Pluto. The scientists think Pluto is simply another one of these objects.

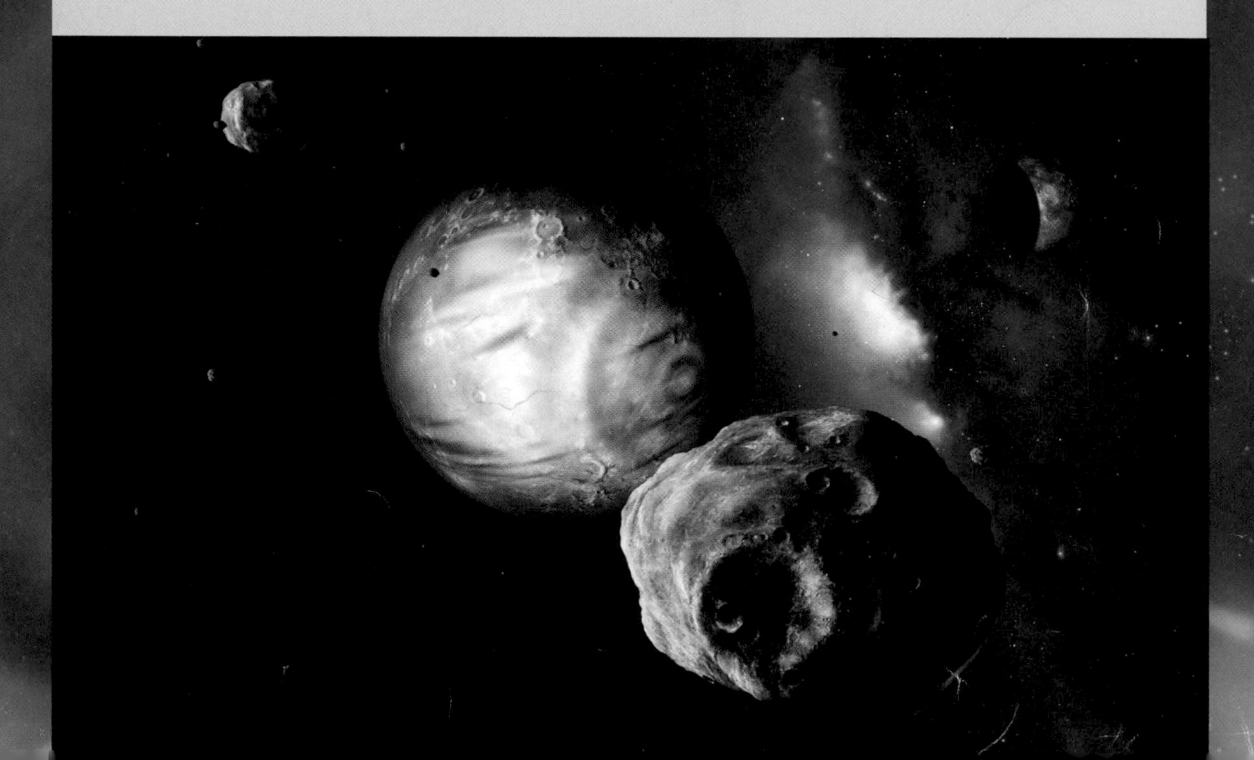

Planet Comparison Chart

Planet	Size Rank (1=largest)	Makeup	1 Trip around the Sun (Earth Time)
Mercury	8	rock	88 days
Venus	6	rock	225 days
Earth	5	rock	365 days, 6 hours
Mars	7	rock	687 days
Jupiter	1	gases and ice	11 years, 11 months
Saturn	2	gases and ice	29 years, 6 months
Uranus	3	gases and ice	84 years
Neptune	4	gases and ice	164 years, 10 months
Pluto	9	rock and ice	248 years

Glossary

atmosphere (AT-muhss-feehr)—the layer of gases that surrounds some planets and moons

axis (AK-siss)—an imaginary line that runs through the middle of a planet; a planet spins on its axis.

core (KOR)—the inner part of a planet that is made of metal or rock

crust (KRUHST)—the thin outer layer of a planet's surface

mantle (MAN-tuhl)—the part of a planet between the crust and the core

spacecraft (SPAYSS-kraft)—a vehicle that travels in space

telescope (TEL-uh-skope)—an instrument that makes faraway objects appear larger and closer

Read More

Birch, Robin. *Pluto.* The Solar System. Philadelphia: Chelsea Clubhouse, 2004.

Goldstein, Margaret J. *Pluto.* Our Universe. Minneapolis: Lerner, 2003.

Rau, Dana Meachen. *Pluto.* Our Solar System. Minneapolis: Compass Point Books, 2003.

Internet Sites

FactHound offers a safe, fun way to find Internet sites related to this book. All of the sites on FactHound have been researched by our staff.

Here's how:

1. Visit *www.facthound.com*
2. Type in this special code **0736836934** for age-appropriate sites. Or enter a search word related to this book for a more general search.
3. Click on the **Fetch It** button.

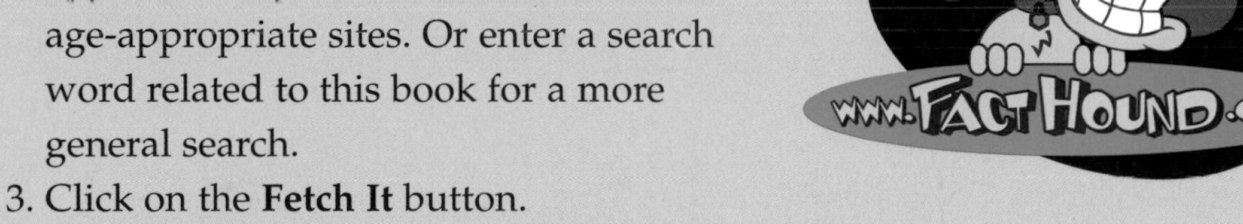

FactHound will fetch the best sites for you!

Index